4. Shake paint (and textile medium) thoroughly before using. Pour a small puddle of paint onto your palette. If you are using acrylic paint and textile medium, pour an equal amount of textile medium next to the paint puddle. Mix the textile medium into the paint thoroughly. If you are mixing colors, be sure to mix them thoroughly too. Have a disposable cup or bowl of water and some paper towels handy to rinse and wipe your brush when necessary.
5. Choose soft, synthetic brushes for painting. Use a flat brush for filling in the larger areas of the design and a small round brush for filling in smaller areas. A thin liner brush will be invaluable for outlining and detailing. Matching size of brush to the size of the area you wish to paint, dip brush into paint being careful not to get too much paint on brush. You don't want to get paint into the metal part of the paintbrush. Wipe any excess paint onto your palette and begin painting your design. Evenly apply a thin, solid coat of paint to each area. Several thin coats of paint may be required to get adequate coverage. Be sure to allow one color to dry before using another color or adding the next coat. It is a good idea to stop and clean your brush occasionally while painting; however, don't leave your paintbrushes standing in water.
6. If paint splatters on your garment, use a paring knife to gently scrape off paint before it dries; remove stain with non-acetone nail polish remover. If this doesn't work, try to gently wash it out with soap and water while the paint is still wet; try not to get the whole garment wet. Even if you can't get the spot out, you can cover it with a button, a bow, a lace motif, or a dimensional fabric paint design.
7. Allow design to dry completely before redrawing any lost outlines or detail lines with a permanent felt-tip pen.
8. Some paints and ... dium require heat-sett... instructions on ... one before adding a... fabric paints to t... g, remove freezer p... apped cardboard or T-shirt form and follow manufacturer's instructions to heat-set painted design.

9. We decorated and personalized some of our garments by adding buttons, bows, ribbons, jewel stones, lace trims, lace motifs, and dimensional squeeze-bottle fabric paint. You can sew or glue the trims to garments and use dimensional paint or glue to adhere jewels. Dimensional squeeze-bottle fabric paints are a bit different than other fabric paints. Read Tips For Using Dimensional Squeeze-Bottle Fabric Paints before applying these paints to your garment.
10. Allow paint to dry at least 72 hours before washing. To launder, turn garment inside out; machine wash on gentle cycle, following paint and/or glue manufacturer's instructions for water temperature. Hang to dry.

TIPS FOR USING DIMENSIONAL SQUEEZE-BOTTLE FABRIC PAINTS

1. Turn the bottle upside down and let paint fill the tip to keep paint flowing smoothly.
2. Clean the tip often with a paper towel.
3. If the tip becomes clogged, insert a straight pin into the opening or remove the tip and clean with warm water.
4. If a mistake is made, use a paring knife to gently scrape off paint before it dries; remove stain with non-acetone nail polish remover or soap and water. Or, camouflage the mistake by incorporating it into the design.
5. Keep painted garment lying flat at least 24 hours to allow the paint to sufficiently set before handling.

OUR PRECIOUS PALETTE

Part of the appeal
of the Precious Moments
children is their unique colors.
Here we've given you the color palette
that we used for our painted garments.

Flesh - 1

Hair - 2 or 3

Clothing - 2, 3, 4, 5, 6, 7, 8, 9, 10, 11,
and white

Shoes - 2, 4, 5, 7, 8, 11, 12, and white

Flowers, umbrellas, birds, animals,
and other details in your design
may be painted any
of the colors.

Love Is Patient

CHAMP
I'm A Possibility

Jesus Loves Me

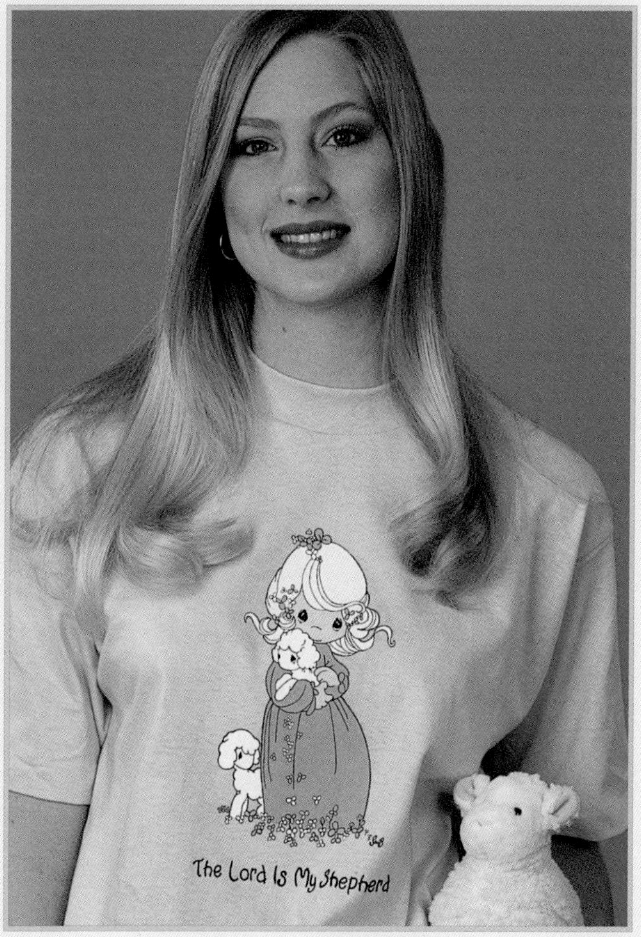
The Lord Is My Shepherd

Jesus Is The Answer
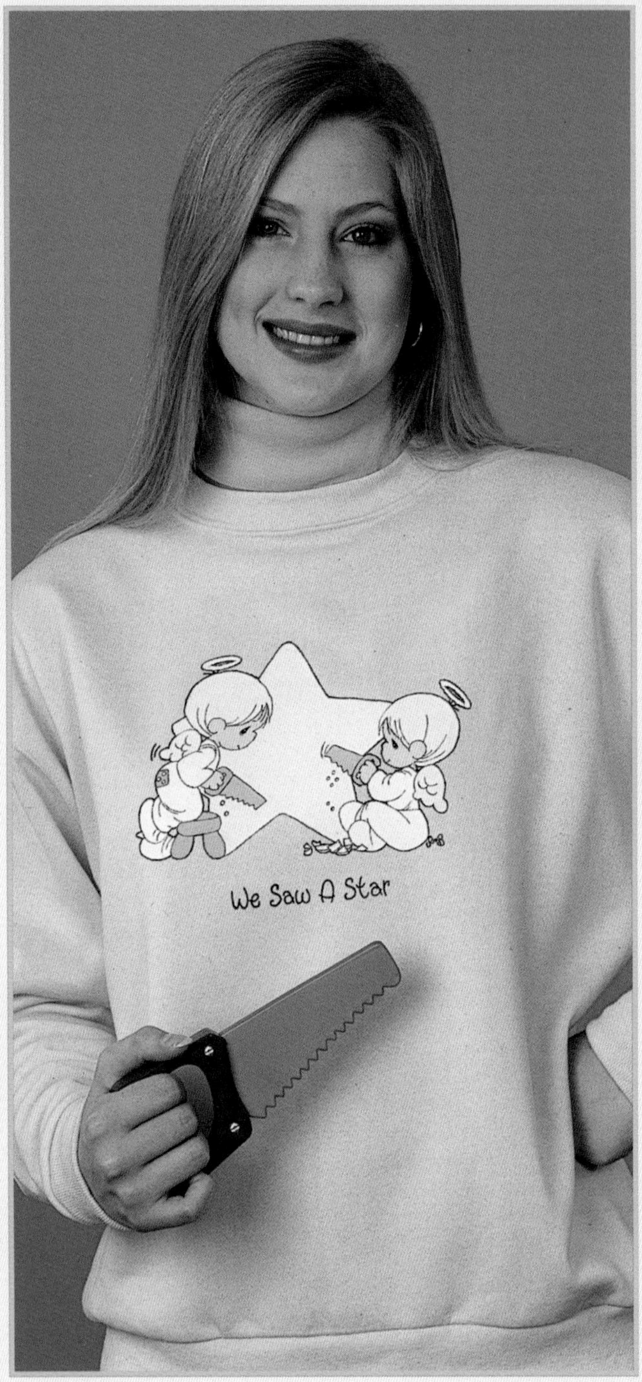
We Saw A Star

Jesus Loves Me

Love One Another

May The Sun Always
Shine On You

You Are Always In My Heart

His Eye Is On The Sparrow

Easter's On Its Way

Peace
On
Earth

God Is Love, Dear

Rejoice

Test Transfer

Make A Joyful Noise

Test Transfer

Jesus Loves Me

Jesus Loves Me

Test Transfer

Love One Another

Test Transfer

Jesus Is The Light

God Loveth A Cheerful Giver

God Loveth A Cheerful Giver

Test Transfer

Love Is Kind

Test Transfer

He Leadeth Me

He Leadeth Me

He Leadeth Me

Test Transfer

Jesus Is The Answer

Jesus Is The Answer

Test Transfer

I Love To Tell The Story

Test Transfer

You Can't Run Away from God

Test Transfer

To God Be The Glory

Test Transfer

Jesus Is The Only Way

Test Transfer

The Lord Is My Shepherd

The Lord Is My Shepherd

Test Transfer

God Is Love

God Is Love

Test Transfer

Onward Christian Soldiers

Onward Christian Soldiers

Onward Christian Soldiers

Test Transfer

Sending You A Rainbow

Sending You A Rainbow

Test Transfer

I Will Make You Fishers Of Men

Test Transfer

Dreams Really Do Come True

Test Transfer

May Only Good Things Come Your Way

May Only Good Things Come Your Way

Test Transfer

His Eye Is On The Sparrow

His Eye Is On The Sparrow

His Eye Is On The Sparrow

Test Transfer

You Are Always In My Heart

Sending You Showers Of Blessings

Test Transfer

There Shall Be Showers Of Blessings

There Shall Be Showers Of Blessings

Test Transfer

I Believe In Miracles

I Believe In Miracles

Test Transfer

High Hopes

High Hopes

High Hopes

Test Transfer

Test Transfer

Thank You For Coming To My Ade

Fresh
Lemonade
Thank You
For Coming To My

Test Transfer

Friendship Grows
When You Plant A Seed

Test Transfer

Good Friends Are Forever

Good Friends Are Forever

Test Transfer

A Friend Is Someone Who Cares

Test Transfer

I'm So Glad That God Blessed Me With A Friend Like You

I'm So Glad That God Blessed Me With A Friend Like You

I'm So Glad That God
Blessed Me With A
Friend Like You

Test Transfer

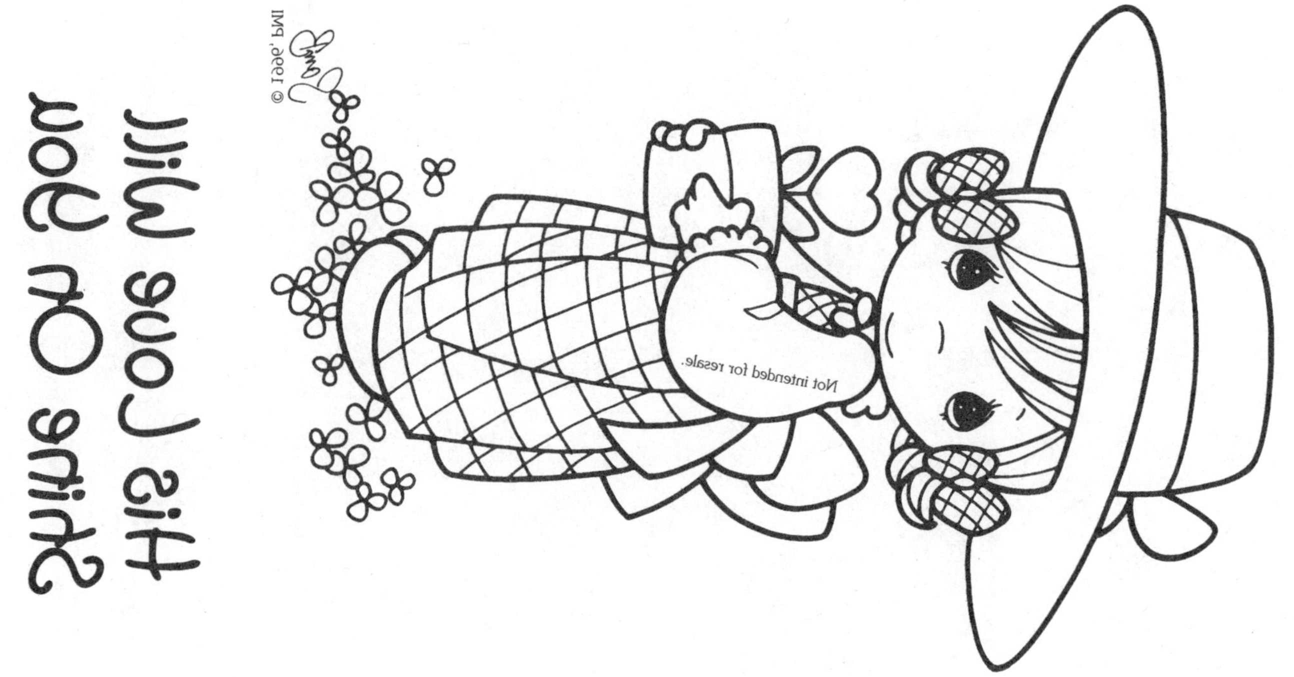

His Love Will Shine On You

You Are My Number One

Test Transfer

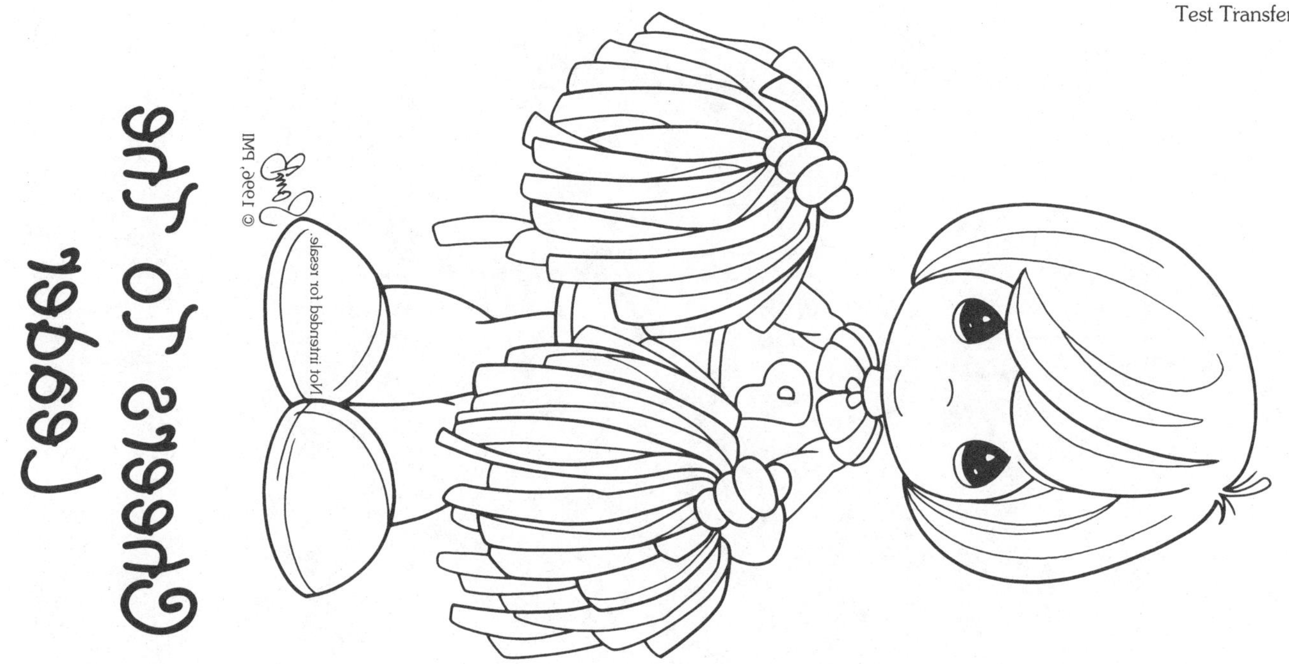

Cheers To The Leader

God Bless You For Touching My Life

Test Transfer

Eggspecially For You

Friendship Hits The Spot

Test Transfer

Test Transfer

Test Transfer

Test Transfer

You Have Touched So
Many Hearts

You Have Touched So
Many Hearts
Sending You My Love

Test Transfer

Sending You My Love

Sending You My Love

Good News Is So Uplifting

Good News Is So Uplifting

Good News Is So Uplifting

Test Transfer

Let Love Reign

Let Love Reign

Let Love Reign

Test Transfer

Love Is Sharing

Test Transfer

Love Is Kind

Love Is Kind

Test Transfer

Hug One Another

Hug One Another

Test Transfer

But Love Goes On Forever

But Love Goes On Forever

Test Transfer

God Bless Our Home

God Bless Our Home

Test Transfer

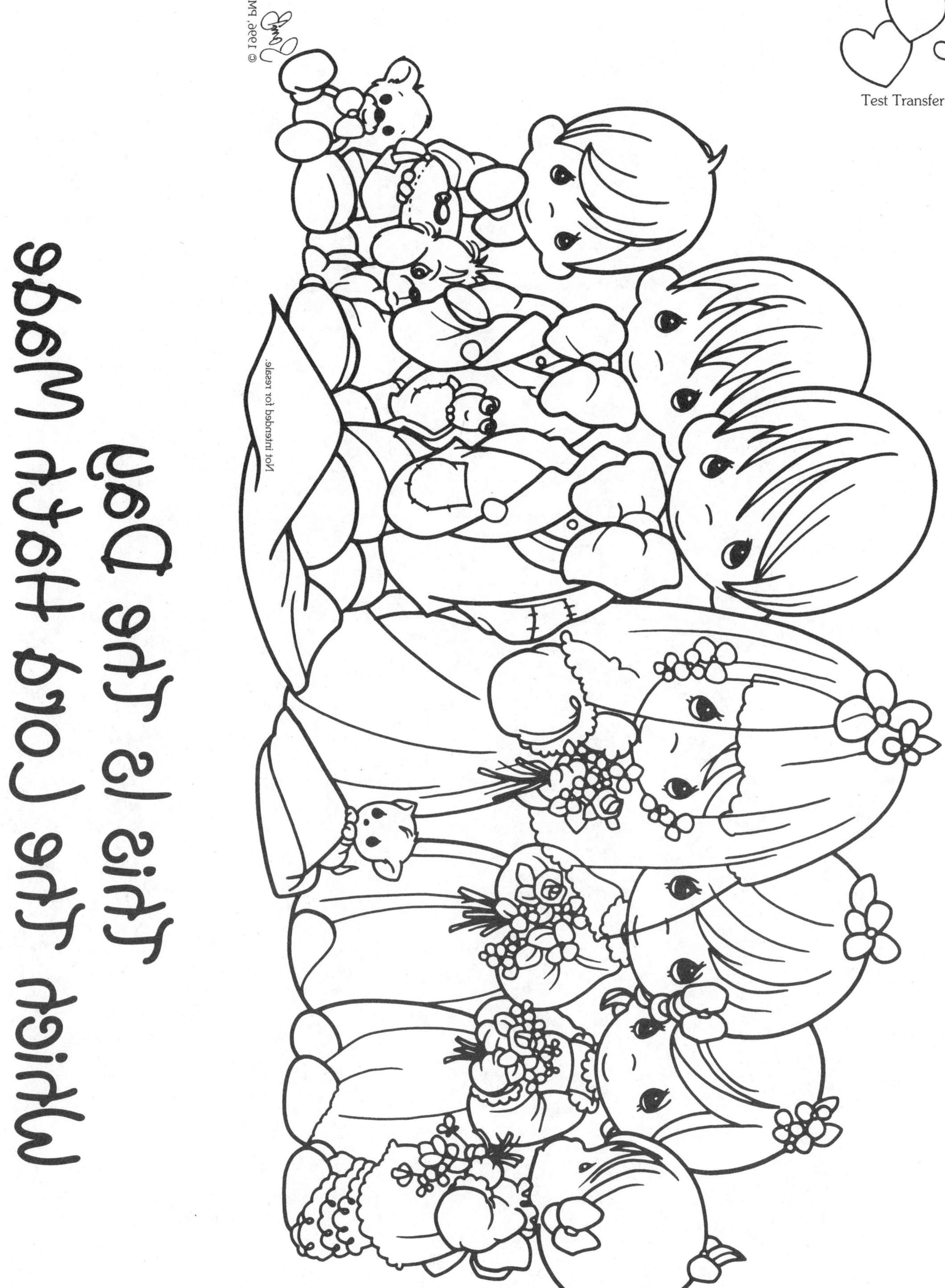

This Is The Day Which The Lord Hath Made

Test Transfer

Not intended for resale.
© 1996, PMI

The Lord Bless You And Keep You

The Lord Bless You And Keep You

The Lord Bless You
And Keep You

Test Transfer

Sharing Our Joy Together

Sharing Our Joy Together

Test Transfer

Wishing You Roads Of Happiness

Bless You Two

Test Transfer

Bon Voyage

Bon Voyage

Test Transfer

Test Transfer

To A Very Special Sister

To A Very Special Sister

Test Transfer

To A Very Special Mom

Mommy, I Love You

Test Transfer

Happy Birthday Poppy

To A Special Dad

Test Transfer

May Your Every Wish Come True

May Your Birthday Be A Blessing

Test Transfer

The Joy Of The Lord Is My Strength

The Joy Of The Lord Is My Strength

Test Transfer

Test Transfer

Test Transfer

Test Transfer

Baby

Test Transfer

Baby's First Step

Test Transfer

Test Transfer

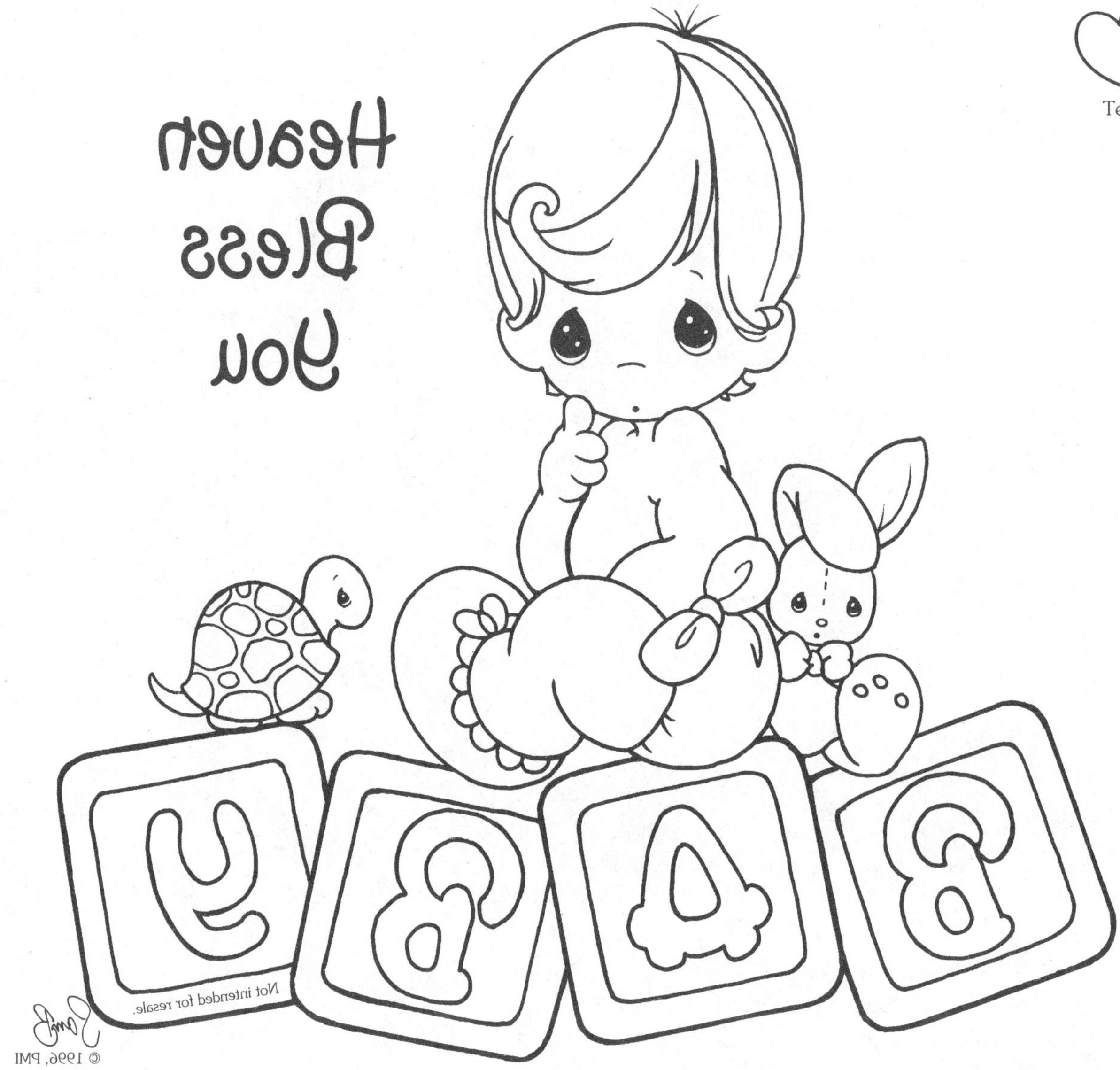

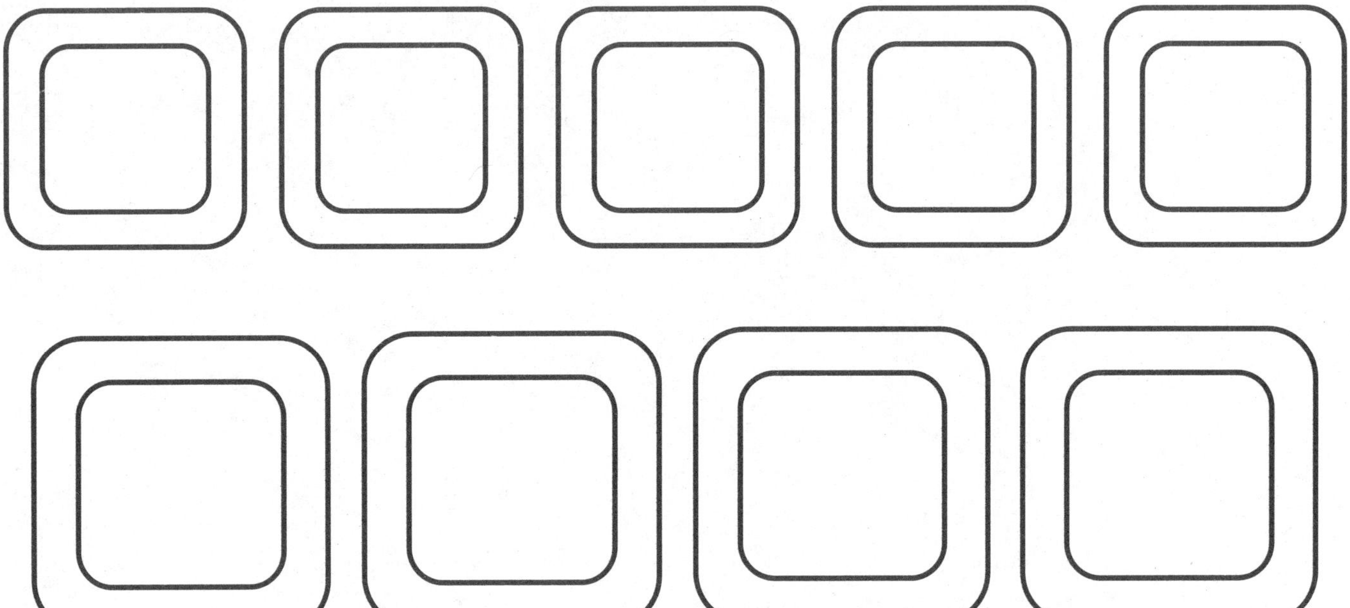

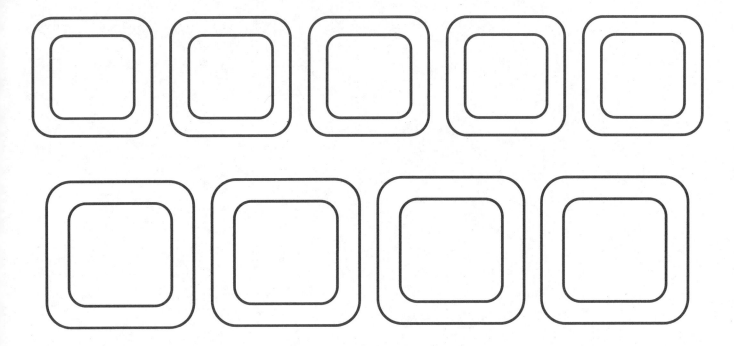

Test Transfer

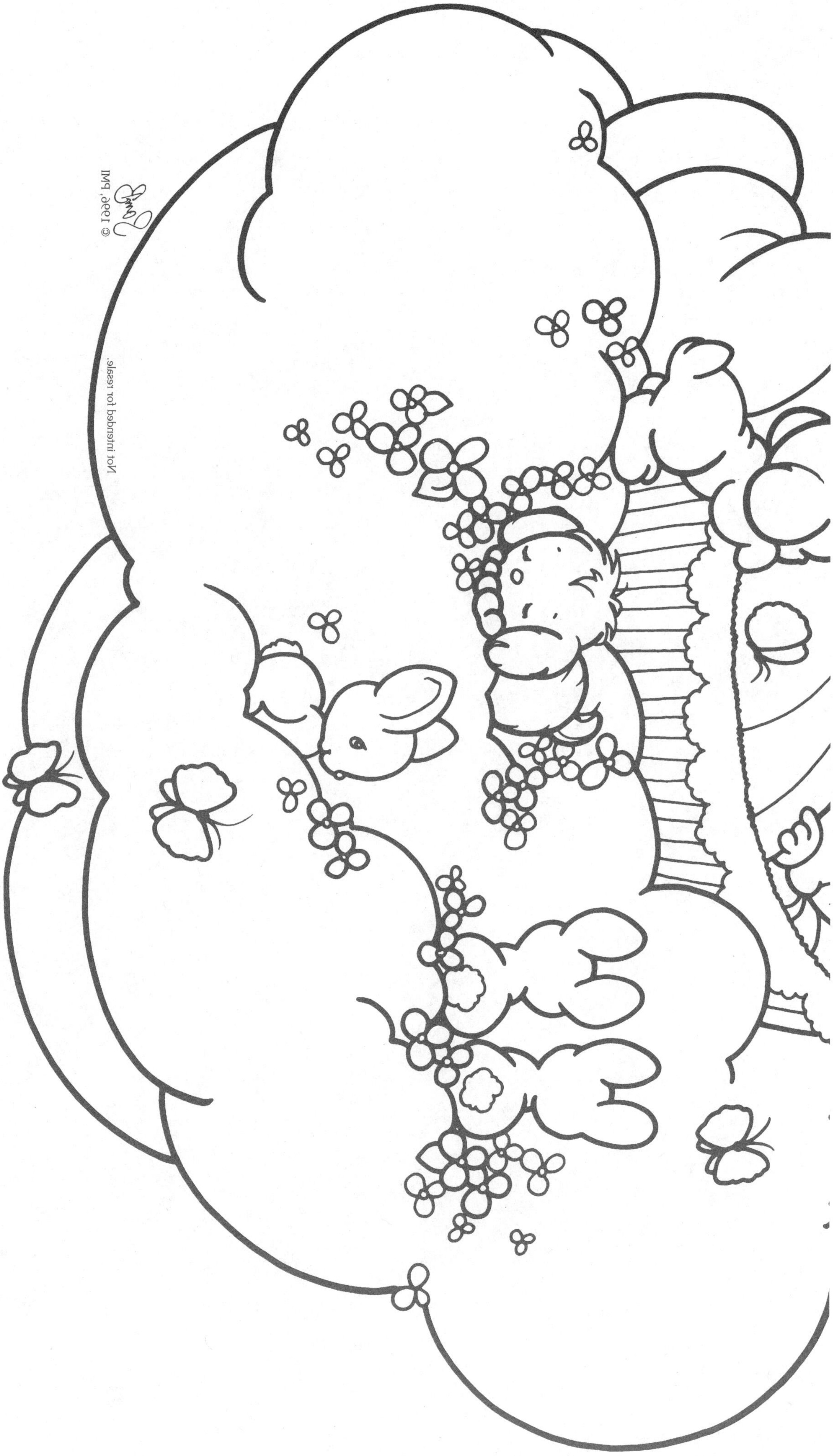
© 1996, PMI
Not intended for resale.

Test Transfer

Safe In The Arms Of Jesus

Safe In The Arms Of Jesus

Test Transfer

Lord Keep Me On My Toes

Lord
Keep Me
On My
Toes

Test Transfer

Lord, Turn My Life Around

Lord, Turn My Life Around

Test Transfer

Test Transfer

I'm A Possibility

Test Transfer

May Your Life Be Blessed
With Touchdowns

May Your Life Be Blessed With Touchdowns

Test Transfer

Pretty As A Princess

Pretty As A Princess

Pretty As A Princess

Test Transfer

Test Transfer

Test Transfer

Hallelujah Country

Test Transfer

Lord Help Me Make The Grade

Happy Days Are Here Again

Test Transfer

Put On A Happy Face

Test Transfer

Happiness Divine

Happiness Divine

Test Transfer

The Lord Bless You And Keep You

Test Transfer

The Lord Bless You And Keep You

Test Transfer

Congratulations, Princess

Test Transfer

God Bless You Graduate

Test Transfer

Make Me A Blessing

Make Me A Blessing

Make Me A Blessing

Test Transfer

Angel Of Mercy

Angel Of Mercy

Test Transfer

To Tell The Tooth
You're Special

Test Transfer

Love Is Patient

Test Transfer

May The Sun Always Shine On You

May The Sun Always Shine On You

Test Transfer

Test Transfer

Test Transfer

Test Transfer

The Voice Of Spring

The Voice Of Spring

Test Transfer

Summer's Joy

Summer's Joy

Test Transfer

Autumn's Praise

Autumn's Praise

Test Transfer

Winter's Song

Winter's Song

Test Transfer

January Girl

January Girl

Test Transfer

February Girl

Reading Girl

Test Transfer

March Girl

March Girl

March Girl

Test Transfer

April Girl

April Gril

Test Transfer

May Girl

May Girl

My Girl

Test Transfer

June Girl

June Girl

Test Transfer

July Girl

July Girl

Test Transfer

August Girl

Test Transfer

September Girl

September Girl

Test Transfer

October Girl

October Girl

Test Transfer

November Girl

November Girl

Test Transfer

December Girl

December Girl

Test Transfer

God Is Love, Dear Valentine

God Is Love, Dear Valentine

Test Transfer

Loving You Dear Valentine

Test Transfer

Easter's On Its Way

Easter's On Its Way

Test Transfer

Wishing You A Basket
Full Of Blessings

Hoppy Easter Friend

Wishing You A Basket Full Of Blessings

Hoppy Easter Friend

Test Transfer

America, You're Beautiful

America, You're Beautiful

Test Transfer

God Bless The USA

God Bless The USA

Test Transfer

Thank You Lord For Everything

Thank You God
for Everything

Test Transfer

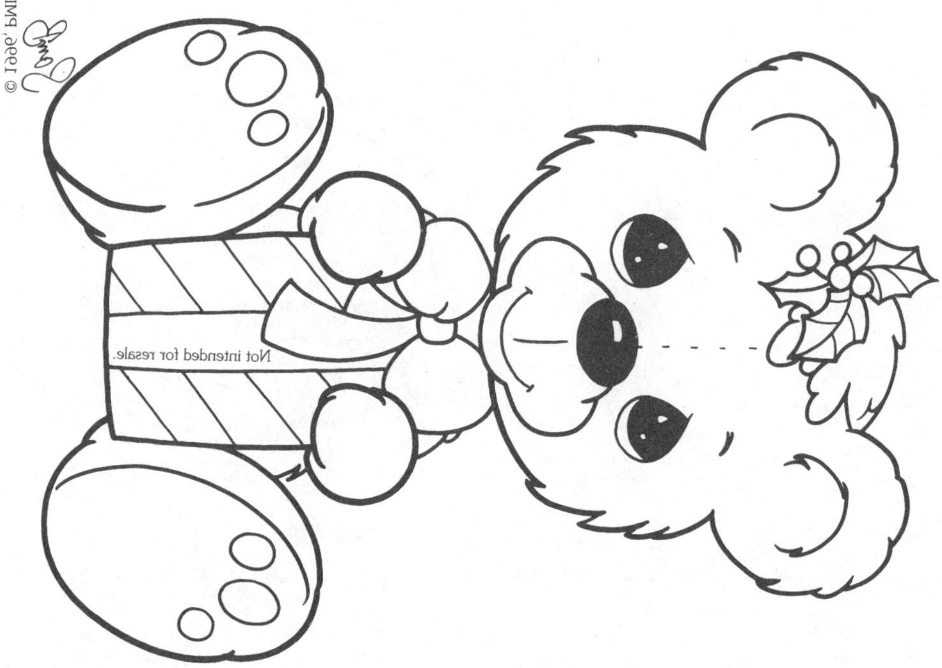

Wishing You A Purr-fect Holiday

Test Transfer

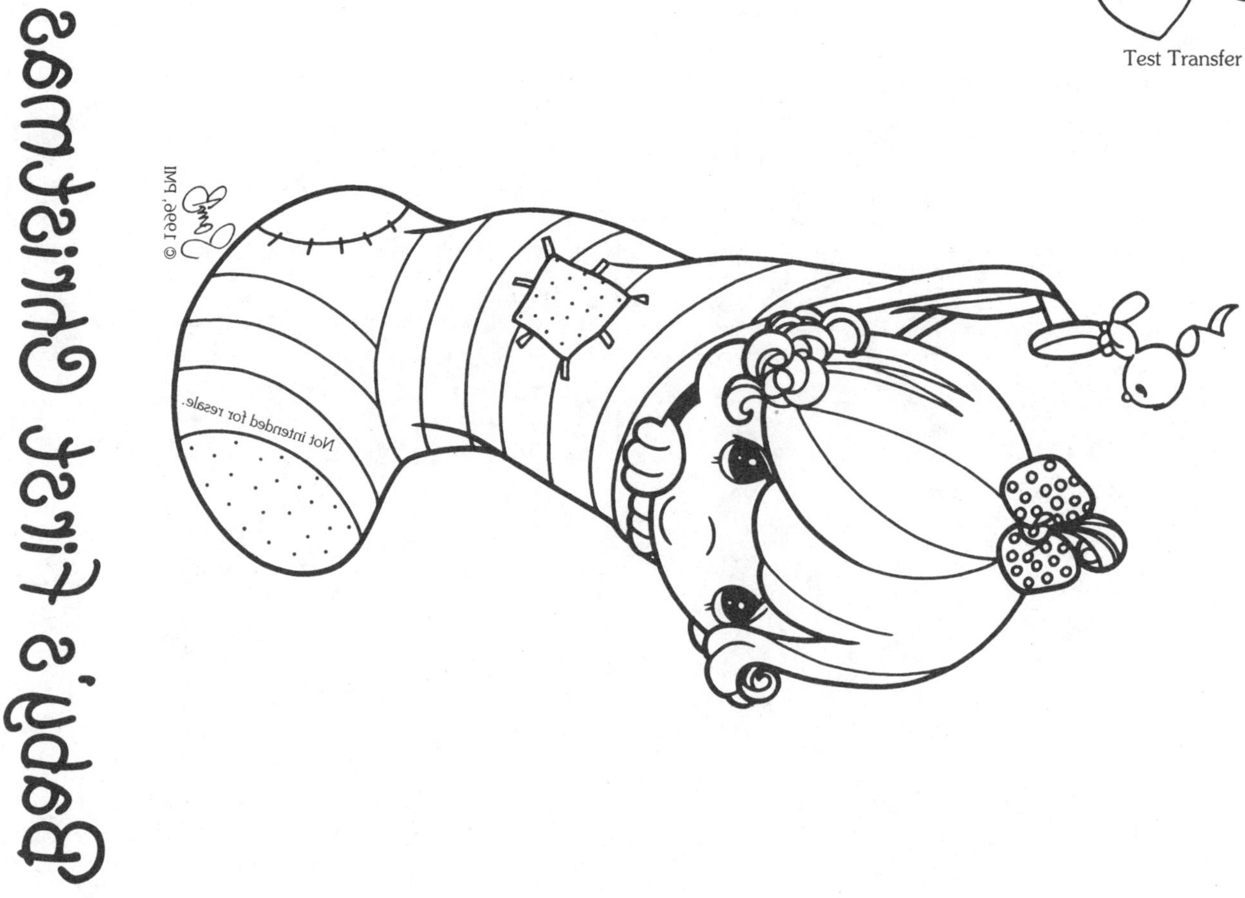

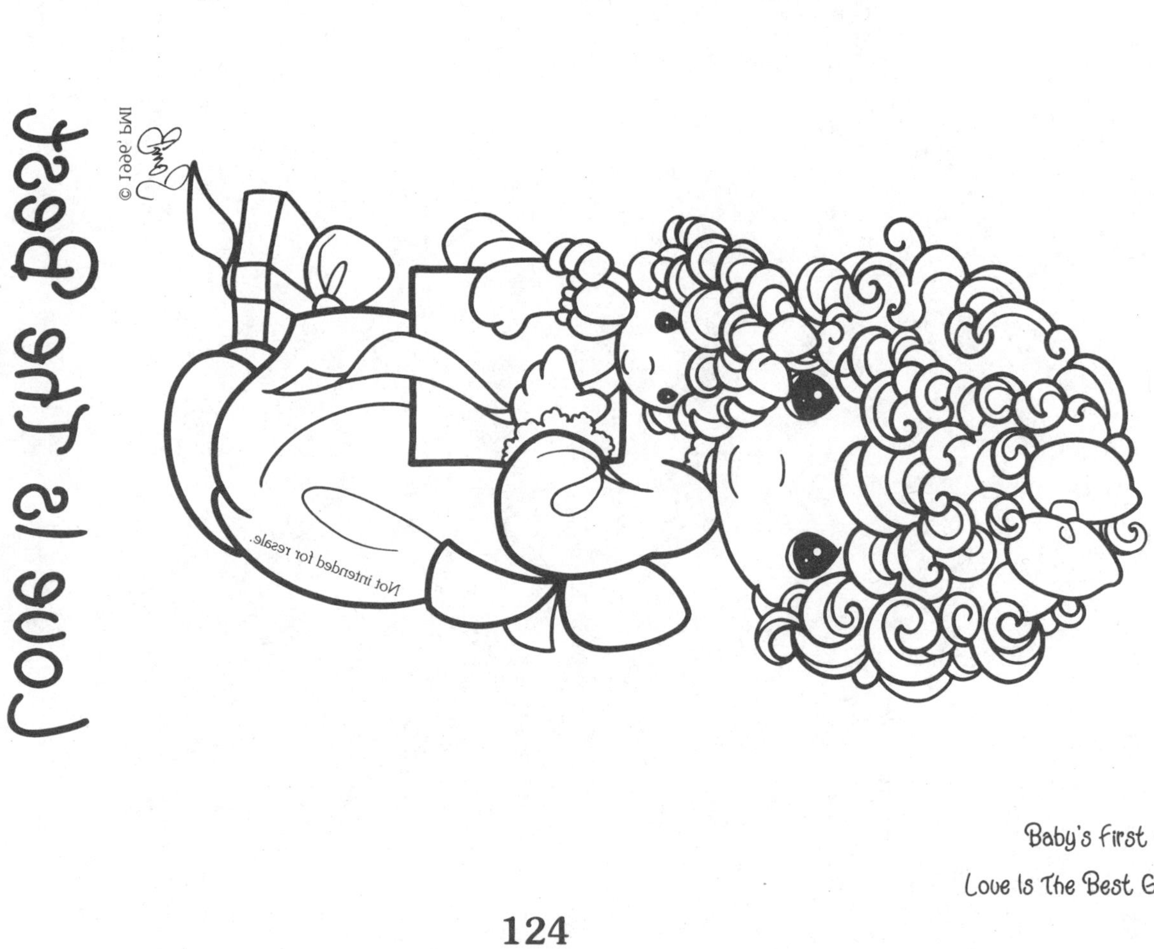

Baby's First Christmas

Love Is The Best Gift Of All

Test Transfer

I'm Sending You A White Christmas

I'm Sending You A White Christmas

Test Transfer

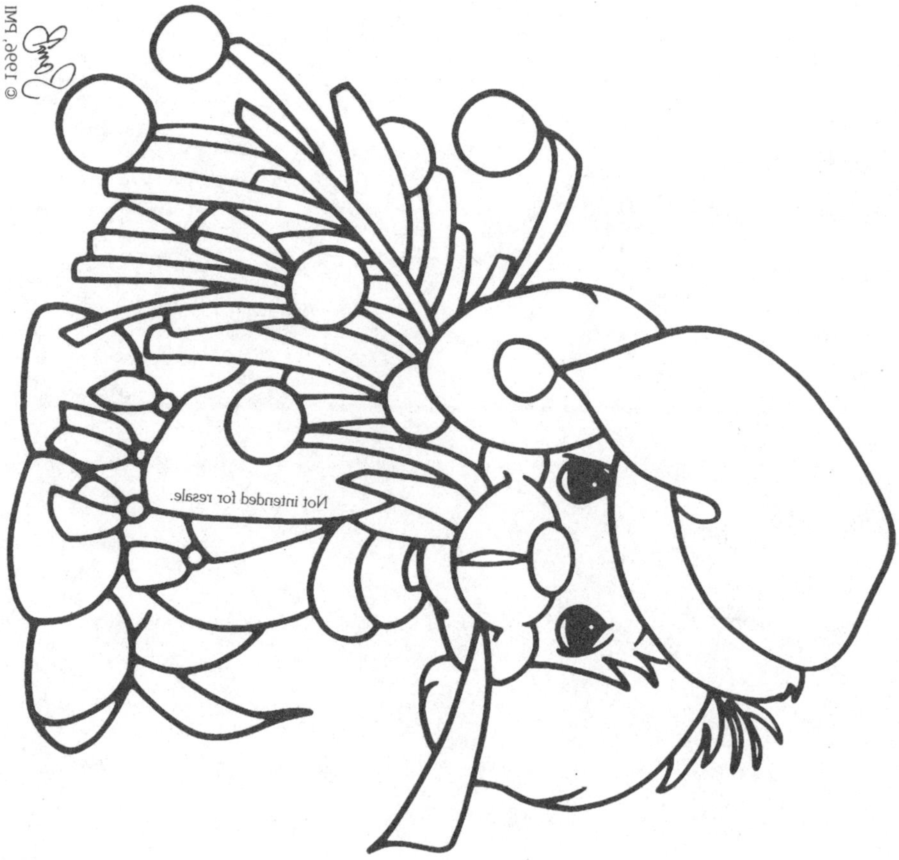

Slow Down
And Enjoy The Holidays

Slow Down And Enjoy The Holidays

Test Transfer

May Your Christmas Be Delightful

May Your Christmas
Be Delightful

Test Transfer

We Saw A Star

Test Transfer

Test Transfer

Peace On Earth

Peace On Earth

Peace On Earth

Test Transfer

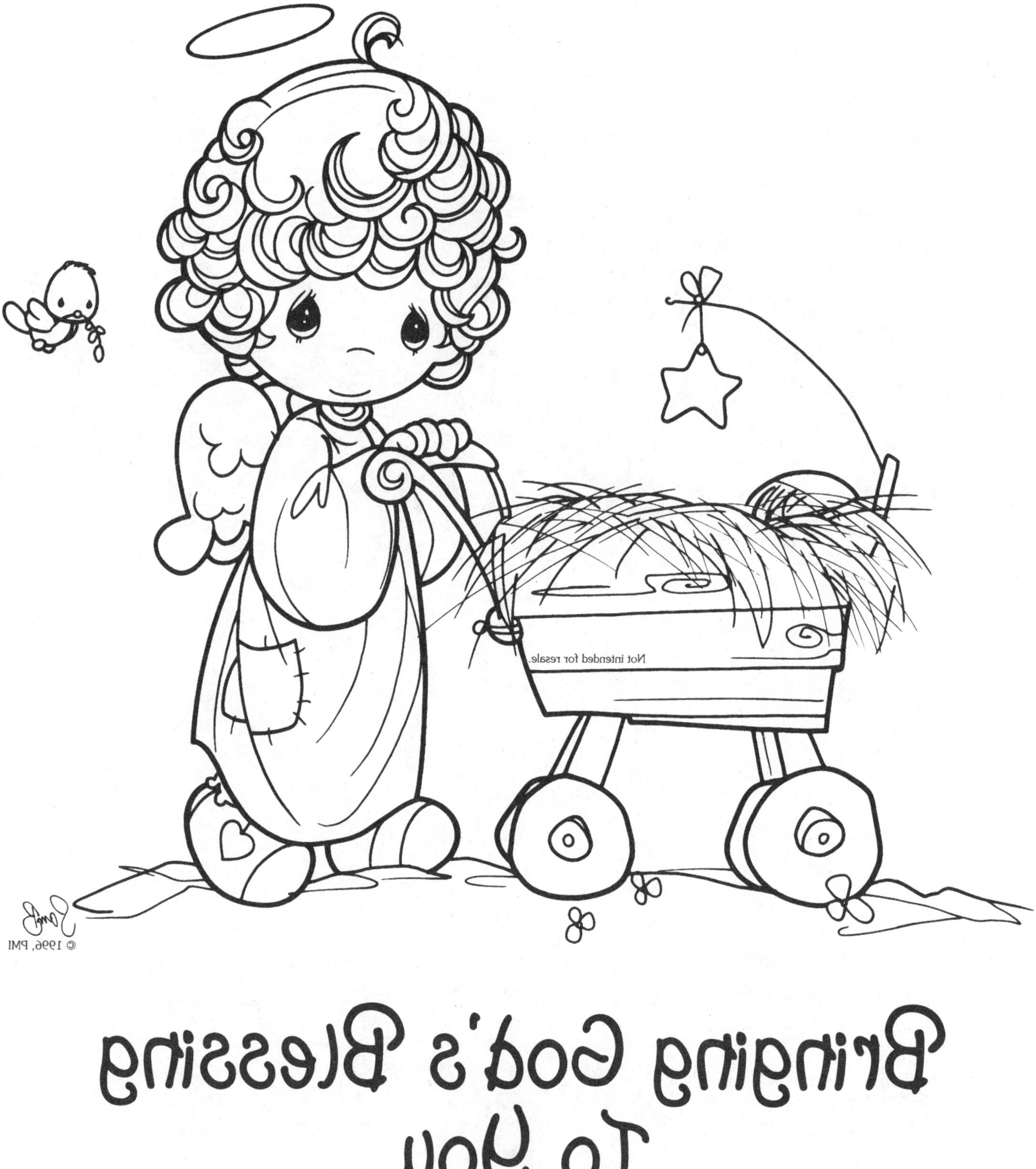

Bringing God's Blessing To You

Bringing God's Blessing
To You

Surrounded With Joy

Test Transfer

I'll Play My Drum For Him

Test Transfer

Let Heaven And Nature Sing

Let Heaven And Nature Sing

Test Transfer

Rejoice O Earth

Rejoice O Earth

Rejoice O Earth

Test Transfer

Peace On Earth

Peace
On
Earth

Test Transfer

Merry Christmas, Deer

Merry Christmas, Deer

Test Transfer

You're As Pretty
As A Christmas Tree

Test Transfer

Wishing You A Ho Ho Ho

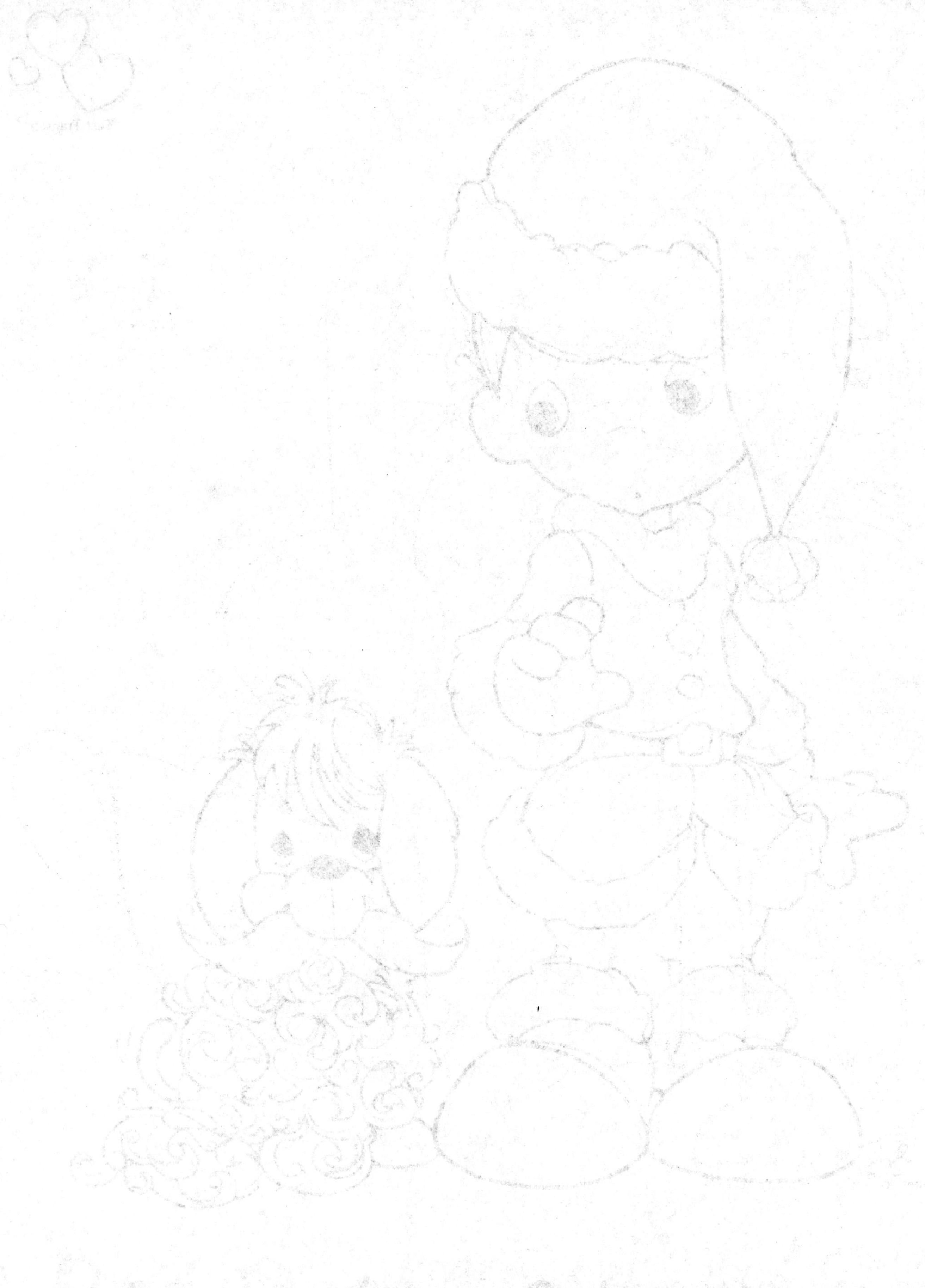
Wishing You A Ho Ho Ho

Test Transfer

Ring Those Christmas Bells

Test Transfer

Do Not Open Till Christmas

Do Not Open til Christmas

Test Transfer

May Your World
Be Trimmed With Joy

May Your World Be Trimmed With Joy

May Your World
Be Trimmed With Joy

Test Transfer

The Wonder Of Christmas

Test Transfer

He Is The Star Of The Morning

He Is The Star Of The Morning

He Is The Star Of The Morning

He Is The Star Of the Morning

© 1996, PMI
Not intended for resale.

Test Transfer

Test Transfer

Test Transfer

Isn't He Wonderful

Isn't He Wonderful

Test Transfer

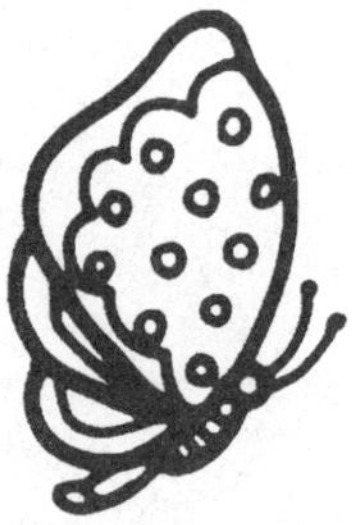

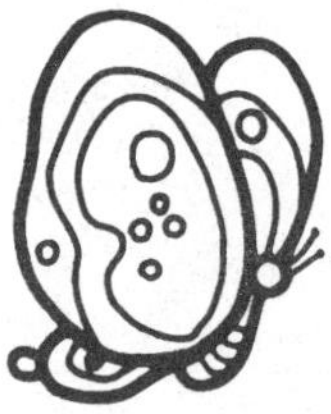

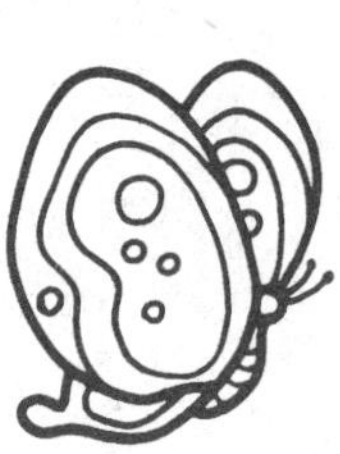

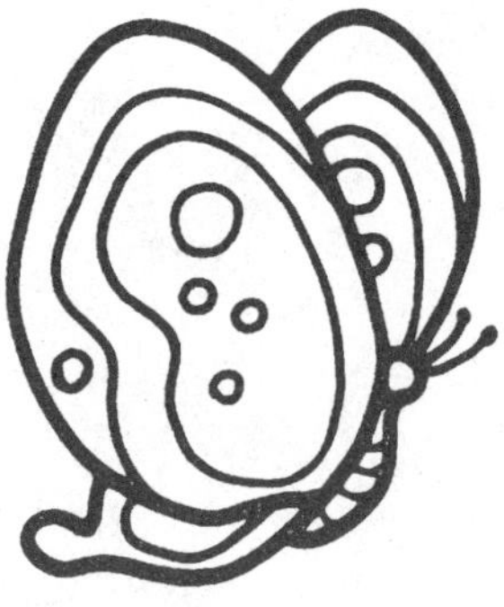

Test Transfer
ZAP!
© 1996, PMI
Not intended for resale.

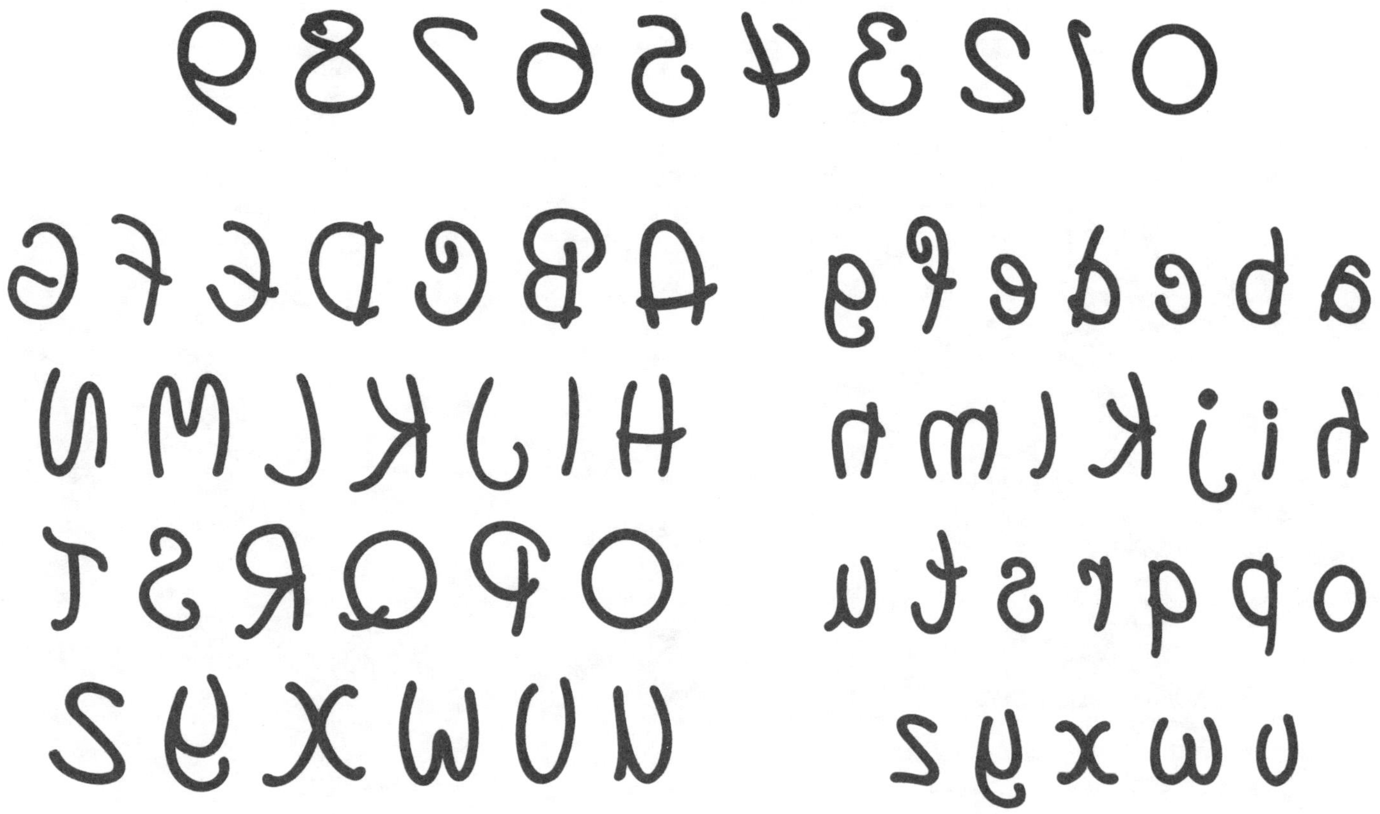

Alphabets and Numbers — We've included several sizes of alphabets and numbers for you to personalize your garments. There is no right or wrong spacing between letters and words; arrange the letters in a manner pleasing to you. To play with the arrangement of letters and words, first cut out the letters you need. Arrange and rearrange letters as you like on your garment, leaving a space for letters used more than once. When you have decided on placement, tape the letters together on the uninked side with Hot Tape. Place words, ink side down, on garment and transfer.

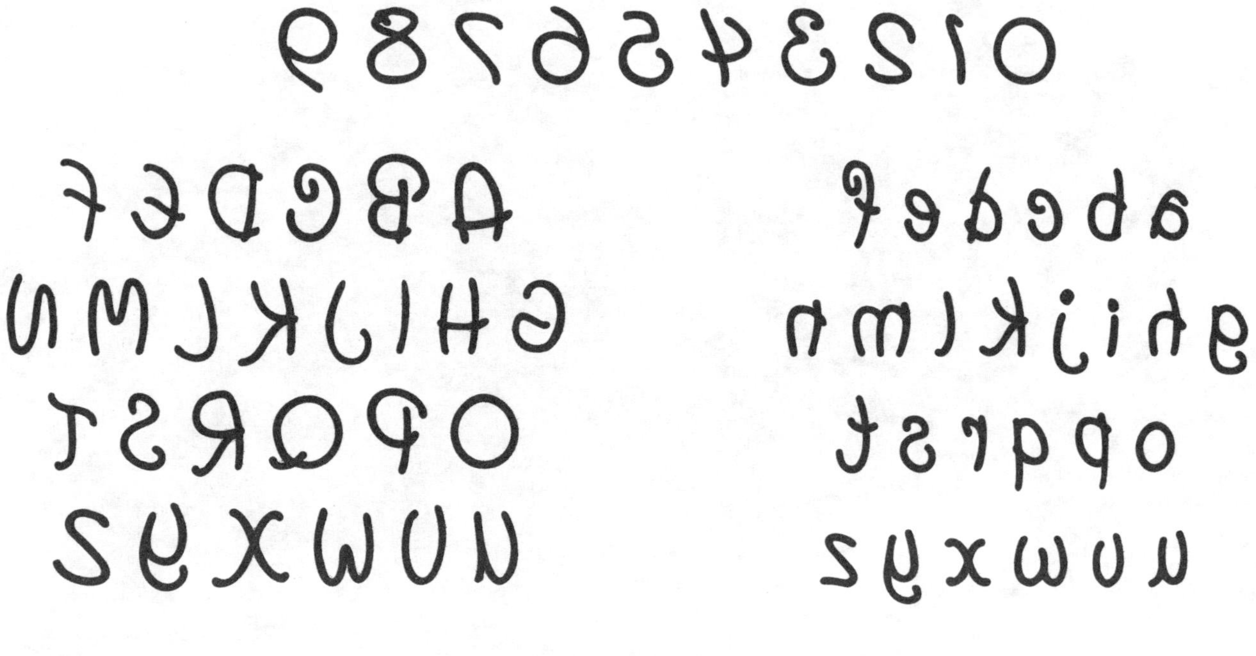

0 1 2 3 4 5 6 7 8 9

a b c d e f g   A B C D E F G

h i j k l m n   H I J K L M N

o p q r s t u   O P Q R S T

v w x y z   U V W X Y Z

Alphabets and Numbers — W[illegible] a place [illegible] personalize your garment. There is no [illegible] words [illegible] letters and words arrange the letters in a [illegible] to play with the arrangement of letters and words [illegible] letters you need. Arrange [illegible] as you [illegible] on your garment [illegible] letters used more than once [illegible] when you have decided [illegible] place [illegible] tape [illegible] with Hot Tape. Place words [illegible] garment [illegible]

0 1 2 3 4 5 6 7 8 9

a b c d e f   A B C D E F

g h i j k l m n   G H I J K L M N

o p q r s t   O P Q R S T

u v w x y z   U V W X Y Z

Test Transfer

A B C D E F G H I J

K L M N O P Q R S

T U V W X Y Z

0 1 2 3 4 5 6 7 8 9

a b c d e f g h i j

k l m n o p q r s

t u v w x y z

0 1 2 3 4 5 6 7 8 9

A B C D E F G H I J
K L M N O P Q R S
T U V W X Y Z

0 1 2 3 4 5 6 7 8 9

a b c d e f g h i j
k l m n o p q r s
t u v w x y z

0 1 2 3 4 5 6 7 8 9

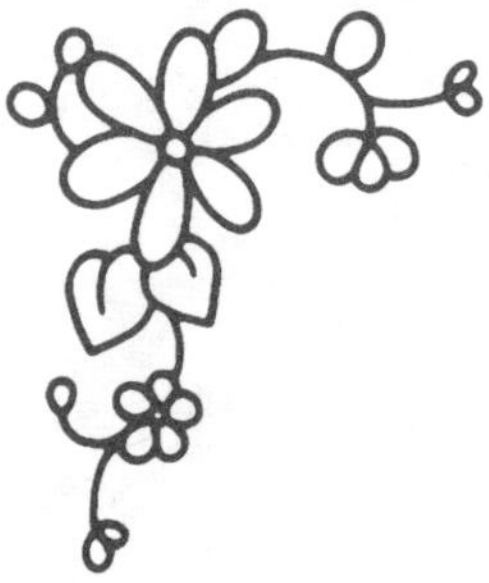

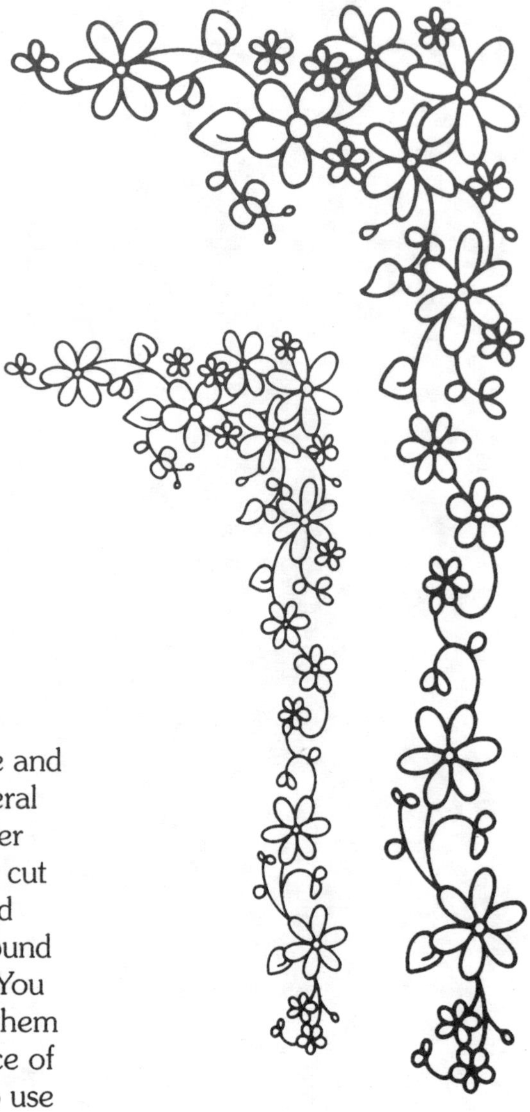

The transfers here and on the next several pages are border designs. You can cut them apart and arrange them around another design. You can also transfer them to a separate piece of fabric or paper to use as a frame for a favorite photo or a painted design.

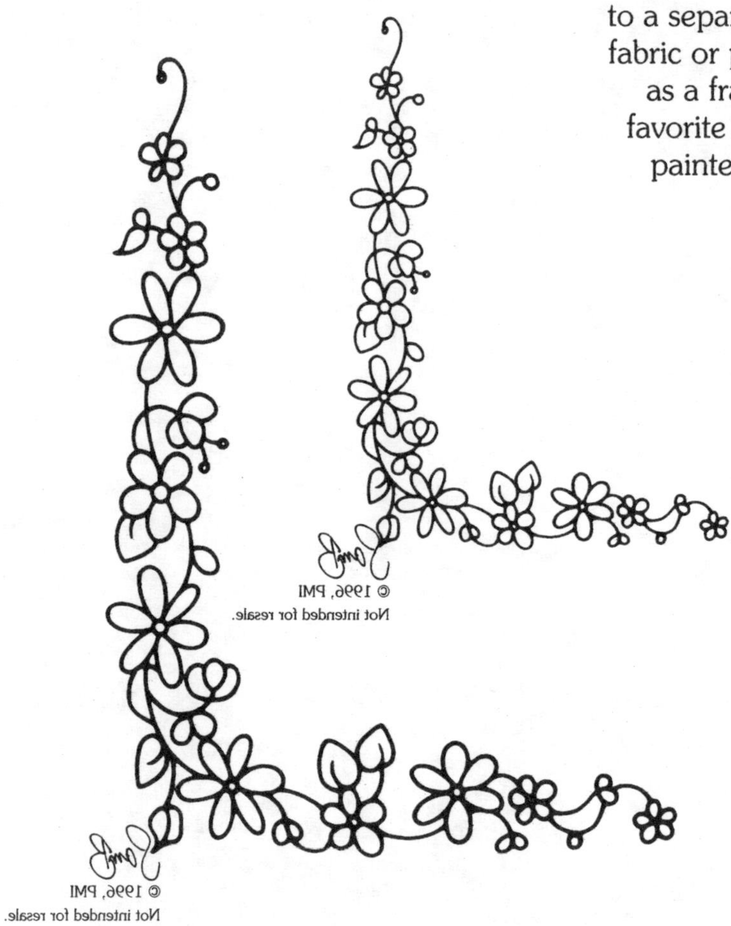

Test Transfer

Test Transfer

Test Transfer

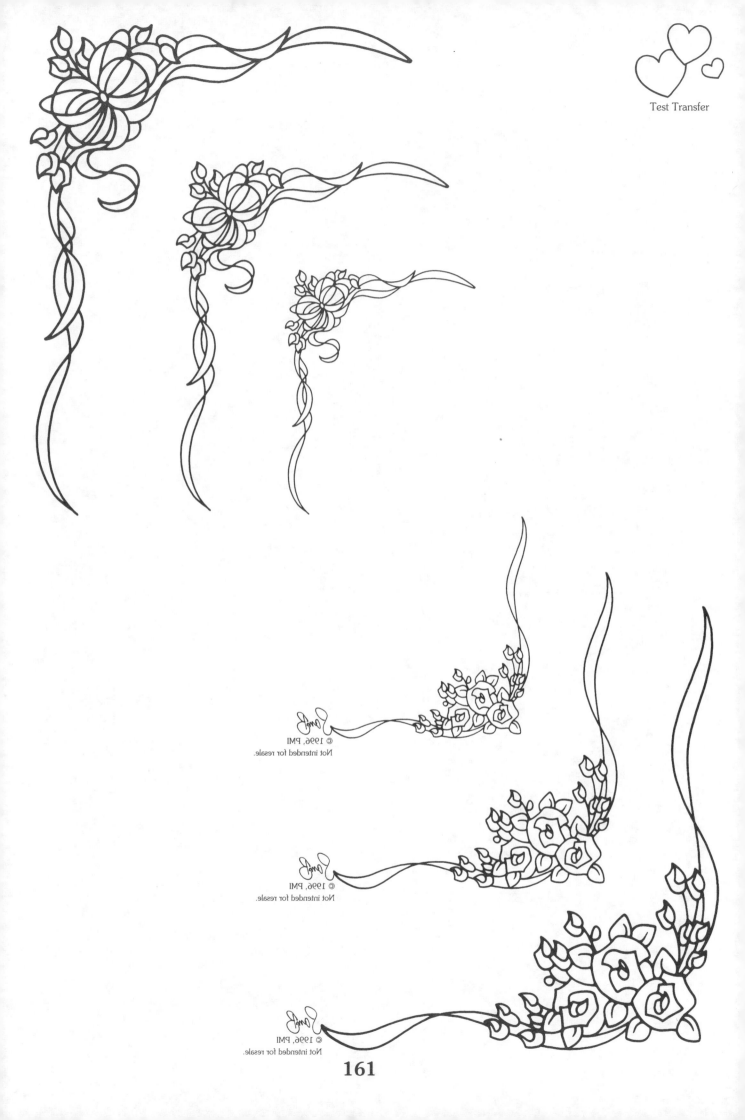

Test Transfer

© 1996, PMI
Not intended for resale.

© 1996, PMI
Not intended for resale.

Test Transfer

Test Transfer

Test Transfer

Test Transfer

Test Transfer

Test Transfer